On The Fence
A WOMAN BETWEEN *PAKISTAN* AND THE *WEST*

Magda Khan

authorHOUSE®

AuthorHouse™
1663 Liberty Drive, Suite 200
Bloomington, IN 47403
www.authorhouse.com
Phone: 1-800-839-8640

First published by AuthorHouse 11/17/2008

ISBN: 978-1-4389-3224-8 (sc)

Printed in the United States of America
Bloomington, Indiana

This book is printed on acid-free paper.

Contents

On The Fence

I call this article "sitting on the fence", because I have a perfect insight into the minds of both parties, and would so much like that all mankind could live in peace, with different views on religion, or life in general, and without wanting to convert the others to their point of view." Live and let live" would make the world a so much better place , with all that money spent on destruction, being used to improve living standard worldwide.

Why the fears and insecurities? Surely there is enough for all of us, if we just learn to share.

There are different reasons for war between countries, or between religions, or between different concepts -

There is lust for fame, land or money
There is fanatism
But last, not least, there is ignorance.

Wars are always planned by the powerful, the governments, and the religious leaders; but suffered by the common people. It is them, the workers, and the farmers, the soldiers, who die, who starve, and who suffer.

The common man is usually content with his life, He is happy, if he earns enough to enjoy a reasonable standard of living; and in the third world, people have enough to do, to make both ends meet, to feed their families. They have no interest in war.

But to start a war, the powerful of this world need the support of the masses. To achieve this, antiheroes are created, lies are circulated, fanatism is fanned, and slogans are concocted.

The public will support the idea of a conflict only, if it is scared of the loss of livelihood, if it fears an attack on its fundamental rights, its ideology.

I am always surprised; at the way public opinion can be swayed by the media in an educated western world, how more so in third-world countries, where education is a privilege of the rich.

I am a western woman, who has lived in Pakistan, and accepted Islam as a perfect way of life, governed by peace. But I have also seen, how small children are brainwashed in the religious "Madrissas" to hate the "infidel", namely Jews and Christians and Hindus, enough to give their young lives for their false ideals. They do so in the firm believe, to do good, to please God, and to earn paradise. This hatred is partly born of suppression by the financially powerful West, of envy of the better, freer life.

The children of the well-off, who can afford the expensive private schools, focus on a good education, on science and business. They have a much wider horizon; they can see the advantages in both systems and its flaws. They dream of getting good jobs, to live lives as good Muslims within a modern society.

It is the children of the dismally poor, who let themselves be dragged into fanatism. Already they have nothing to loose, a dismal life awaits them, hunger, disease, misery. So why not sacrifice this worthless life for, as they believe, Islam and the downfall of the enemies of Islam?

So, if the West would spend on education, instead of armament; on help to built up a local infrastructure for business in third world countries, not only would they make friends out of enemies, but also people would stay in their own countries, therefore not clogging the social systems of industrialized countries.

Introduction

It was early in the year 1960. I was just 22 years old and on my first flight to London. I had one year in a French-speaking boarding school behind me, and had got a first position in an apprentice. Now I intended to improve my English by spending at least a year in UK. My plan was, to later work in an office. Little did I know that my destiny came to meet me in the form of an oriental prince-charming.

Just one year later I was married to a Pakistani young man, happily planning for a future in his country.

So now, after 40 years of marriage and a difficult but not unhappy life in Pakistan, I have decided to write a few of the unusual things I have lived. I want to leave all that is personal out, as this would make an entire different story.

I have recently seen people who found some postcards, or some writings by their grandparents, or parents, and found that quite interesting. Therefore I have finally decided to tell a bit of my story. Maybe my grandchildren would like to know later on, how I have lived in a so much different society. Maybe even my children don't know everything.

It is now the year 2008, and I am 70 years old, another cause of my failing memory. And then I have lived so many strange things, that a lot of it just disappeared---maybe not enough space on my hard-disk!

People you might find in my writings:

Afzalmy --- husband
Ammi and Bahu-jee   ---- Afzal's parents
According to age:
Masooda, Rasida, Khalida and Azra --- his sisters,
Saeed, Anwar, Akbar and Parvaiz --- his brothers

Yasmin, Samina, Zarina, Naureen --- my daughters
Shahid --- my son

So enjoy whatever I have to tell!

Arrival

It was a wonderful cruise from England to Karachi, through the Suez-canal, into the Indian Ocean. We did nothing but lazing around, eating and dancing in the evenings. The weather was getting hot, even in December.

The arrival in Karachi was very interesting for me: the heat, so many unused noises, people and scents. Afzal had to go through the customs and find our entire luggage, while I was waiting in a kind of waiting room with Yasmin, who was 6 months old. She was a lovely baby with blue eyes and white skin, and chubby cheeks from the healthy sea-air, and attracted the attention of lots of people. All of a sudden, a pock-marked, tall and dark man came towards us. This is my brother Akbar, I was told. He picked up the baby right away, and they seem to understand each other at once.

After a long and tiring wait we proceeded towards the home of the elder sister Rashida. To adapt myself to the local customs I had sewn a shalwar-kamiz in cotton, because I did not want to look different. But I could have saved myself the trouble. Firstly I was stared at by everyone, for my blond hair and blue eyes, and secondly cotton was not at all accepted here. Only poor people wore cotton--- it had to be some kind of nylon or artificial silk.

Karachi at the time--- it was Dec 1961 --- was an overcrowded place, capital of a new country, it lacked badly in accommodation. Walking through the by lanes you found hut like houses which belonged to Doctors or officials. The brother-in-law was working in the railways, and had some very poor quarters in the railway-colony. It was actually 2 servant quarters, joint by a common, small yard. Each of them had one room with a veranda, and across the tiny yard a cubicle without roof or door, only a curtain stretched across the opening. In one of them we took our ablutions, the other was meant for toilet. The cleaning woman came once a day to take away the refuse. I was given the special treatment to be allowed to use this "toilet" right after it was cleaned. We, as the guests were also given one room, where a 2nd cot was added at night. The rest of the family slept in the other room. How they managed I never learnt. It was the family with 4 boys, mother, a brother and a younger sister of my husband that is 5 adults and 4 children. The rooms were really tiny, and I don't know how they squeezed everybody in. The cooking was done in the veranda, on a tiny kerosene-stove, on the floor, sitting on a "piri"- a small stool. The washing in the "bathroom": crouching, with soap-cakes, cold water and a stick to beat the soaped clothes. Luckily we stayed there only for a few days.

Everyday we went out to see the City. A ride in a "Victoria"-- a carriage pulled by a horse was very romantic for me. For these outings my younger sister-in-law, Azra, dressed me in her better clothes. They did not fit, as she was taller than me, were also un-ironed and often stained. I felt like disguised, but went along, trying to make friends.

One day we visited another, older half-sister who lived in a proper house. She invited us to stay with her, but there were some family-politics, which forbade this. During the meal, the children of the neighbours tried to get a glimpse of the newly arrived "mehm sahib", and the family had all the pain to keep chasing them from the windows.

The second day already, I got my first taste of Malaria-fever. I had to take quinine and was given huge glasses of buffalo-milk, to lessen the effect of the medicine. It was very greasy, and to me tasted terrible. After some days (I can't remember how many) we had to leave for Lahore.

Afzal wanted to stay on in Karachi to give some interviews, regarding a job. But he was persuaded to go along, as the wedding of the elder brother Anwar was soon to be celebrated.

We were also informed that my father-in-law was very angry with Afzal for marrying an "infidel, white woman" and had forbidden his family to go and receive us, so the mother sneaked out behind his back--after all she had not seen her son for over 8 years.

I was terrified! How will I be received by the father, will he accept me, or will we have to move out? I insisted for the first time, to wear my own shalwar-kamiz, even though it was cotton. The journey by train lasted around 20 hours. A tight compartment with wooden seats-no chance to sleep, so when we arrived, sleepy and me with swollen eyes from weeping, it was a nice surprise to find Anwar on the station with flower-garlands. The younger brother, Parvaiz was also there.

Anwar brought us home in a car, through what I thought at the time, terrible quarters. Bahu-jee put his hand on my head, therefore accepting me. Yasmin smiled at him and held on to his beard, so the ice was broken. Afzal hugged his father and asked for forgiveness, so all was well.

The house they lived in temporarily was very somber, cobbled floors of two rooms, opening onto the back, with only one window. There was practically no furniture. One slept on cots which were stood in the back porch during the day. But that was only for a day or two, as we shifted into the newly constructed house nearby.

All New Beginning is difficult

The first few months were not easy for me. Not only were the customs new and unusual to me, I also had to learn the language. Here are just a few things I had difficulty with:

Yasmin: My baby slept of course in her cot, at least for the first few nights. But my mother-in-law did not approve. She kept taking the baby out of her bed and putting her in with me. I was of course scared to sleep with a small baby next to me, but after a while I gave up, and I must say, that it is much more natural for a child to sleep with his mother. Also a mother's sleep is so light, that she wakes as soon as the baby wakes. It is also easier to feed during the night, because there was no question of having regular feeding-times. Babies in Pakistan are fed on demand and that day and night. Napkins as such were not available, not to speak of pampers. Without washing machine it was quite a job to wash them, and dry them, especially when it rained. In the beginning we had to tear up some sheets to help out. I already mentioned that washing was done on the floor, with soap cakes, and a stick to beat the dirt out of the clothes.

Beds: The string-cots which were commonly used then, and are still widely used in the villages, felt very uncomfortable to me, and it took me time to get used to them.

Cooking: The first summer we spent in Lahore with my in-laws. Ammi-jan went to Khalida, to help her out for the birth of a baby. So I was the only woman in the house, and was expected to do the cooking, as Azra also went along. The cooking was done in earthen cooking-pots, called handy. And the stove we had then was a tiny charcoal-stove, standing on the floor, and the person who did the cooking was sitting on a piri. Just to light the fire, for me, was an ordeal. Then I was not very well trained in cooking curries. One day, babu-jee tried to show me how to cook. He spoke a few words of English and kept saying, you must roast the meat. As he did not see well, he did not notice, that the meat was burning. And he did not let me add water. Also the chapattis were very difficult to make. Already the dough--- to make soft, thin and nicely round chapattis, the dough has to be kneaded well, not too hard and not too soft. I think it took me more than a year to make them really nice.

Crockery: Crockery at that time was washed with a piece of cloth and some ashes out of the stove. I must say, that the cooking-pots were nice and shining, but my hands got all black.

In summer everyone slept on the roof. The rooms were much very hot, and on the roof there was always a bit of wind. Together with the fans it became bearable. Later, in Tando and Hyderabad we slept in the courtyard, as in Sindh the nights are cool, because it is desert-area. Of course, with this arrangement there is no privacy at all.

I also remember that one day I wanted to help, and filled the water-pitcher. But I must have done something wrong, because ammi emptied it again, washed it thoroughly and refilled it. Drinking water was kept in earthen pitchers, which kept it cool, and gave it a nice taste. In the beginning I boiled all my drinking water. But it never cooled enough, so I stopped with the result that I got diarrhea. Of course, once we got our fridge, the problem was solved.

The Wedding

The preparations for the wedding of my brother-in-law Anwar were in full swing. Every day Afzal and Anwar went to the bazaars, to buy things, like cloth, jewellery and, make-up articles for the bride. Sometimes I was allowed to come along. I enjoyed the noisy, colourful atmosphere of an Asian bazaar. Sometimes we ate also at a small roadside restaurant, all the spicy, delicious foods, sometimes it was ice-cream or "Kulfi". Afzal also bought some fabric for me to sew in all haste some Pakistani dresses. I received presents of gold-jewellery from Anwar and Rashida. To wear my earrings at the wedding I had to have my ears pierced. Usually this was done to small girls by their elders, with a needle and thread. But I got a special treatment; we went to a doctor who pierced my ears with a hypodermic needle, quite to his amusement. This did not stop my ears from getting badly infected, and I suffered quite a bit at the wedding.

I felt very bothered by all the attention I got. Westerners were not an everyday sight in those days, before the young hippies and the tourists started to arrive. So I attracted the curiosity of the crowds, and of course also of the numerous beggars one could find everywhere. This was also very annoying for my husband, when people asked:" where is she from?" or "is she your wife?" He used to get angry, and a quarrel would start, really a very awkward situation for everyone.

So more and more often I was left at home. As I could not speak the language, and my parents-in-law did not speak English, I was very bored. Mostly I stayed on the roof, looking down at the traffic and all the comings and goings. Nobody ever reproached me. It was only much later that I learned, that decent women were not to be seen from the streets. But to me it was amusing.

All the unknown and unusual food, fruits and sweets, gave me a terribly upset stomach. I spent a big part of my days and nights in the toilet, luckily it was a proper flush toilet this time. Poor Yasmin also started losing her lovely pink cheeks, as with my illness the milk dried up, and no powder milk for babies being available, I fed her with the usual, diluted buffalo milk. It did not suit her, and she also became ill. I spent lots of time in washing napkins, pampers were not yet invented. The weather started being rainy and cold, they would not dry, and something like baby-napkins not being available in the shops, we were both in trouble. Of course we saw a doctor for both of us, but I can not remember how long it took to cure us both. I remember still months later, I could eat nothing else but boiled rice with a bit of yoghurt, and my poor baby the same.

The evenings the family gathered, as is the custom still before weddings, to sing and dance. At first I was fascinated, but as the days wore on, the jokes I could not understand, the singing and dancing became monotonous. My nerves were on edge, and the harmless teasing towards me, was often misunderstood, leading to angry differences with Anwar.

The day of the wedding I was very excited. Early morning I was told that the "barat" would soon leave for the bride's house, so I should get ready. I had gotten a beautiful shalwar-kamiz of velvet, all embroidered for myself, and of course also new finery for Yasmin. So I was all ready at the appointed time. A wedding band arrived and played the latest film-songs, unknown to me. The Shenais and the drums were very loud, and it sounded horrible to me; tearing at my already weakened nervous system. I still abhor wedding-bands. For me it sounds a bit like the music they play here at carnival. But now I know at least what they are supposed to play.

I was all ready to go, but nobody else seemed to be. My sister-in-law, Rashida asked me, if I could assist her with her clothes. The Shalwar was too wide, could I sew it quickly for her. Of course, I agreed, took out my electric sewing machine and obliged. As I was doing so, she brought me 2 or 3 more shalwars; as I was on it, could I also do these? I was panicking-- were we not supposed to leave right away? This sewing surely could wait. How could I know, that at weddings time stands still, and a barat expected at 12, will usually only arrive where 2 or even 3 o-clock for lunch. So, with all the tension and the noise, the unheard of happened. I shouted at my father-in-law!!! He only asked me to give some money to the band, as was custom, but my husband not here, I did not understand. Was I supposed to sew or were we not about to leave? So I shouted something and retired to my room. How terribly rude of me!

I do not remember how the wedding proceeded; I was at the end of my tethers, it was all noisy and stressful, late food, crying babies, shouting men and gossiping women probably, like all weddings in those days.

Of course, the dressed up bride, the customs and colours of a Pakistani wedding being new to me, I must have enjoyed also, but I truly do not remember.

Tando Mohammad Khan

With all the comings and goings for the wedding, the picnics and other festivities, time passed, and Afzal had no real time to look for work. It turned out, that the money we had brought from UK was after all not enough to start a small business, as he really wanted to. Also an interview arranged in London for a job as accountant with a multinational did not materialize. So what to do now?

Anwar and his older sister, Masooda were living in East Pakistan, which is now Bangladesh. They had invested in a trucking business here in West Pakistan, which did not seem to go well at all. They suspected the manager to cheat them. So they proposed Afzal to become their employee, and check the accounts of the firm. Afzal agreed right away. He was to get a decent salary, and I was glad to travel with him to Hyderabad, where the business was situated. We stayed in Hyderabad cantonment, in the house of an army-officer, friend to my brother-in-law. As we were supposed to live there only a few months, we borrowed the little essential furniture. My husband hired for me the first servant, a young man from a village nearby, who was to help me with the cleaning and the cooking. Cleaning, in Pakistan, means sweeping the floors with a "jaroo", by crouching on the floor, so as not to swirl up all the dust. A "jaroo" is a bundle of a kind of reed. Then the whole floors have to be wiped with a wet cloth and that every day. In those days that was also done by crouching, and wiping by hand. As we were living outside the town, in a desert area, the frequent sand-storms were an ordeal. One had to quickly close all doors and windows, but even then the fine sand managed to enter everything, clothes, even food. And of course the dusting afterwards!

One month after his arrival it was Eid, and of course the young servant had to go to his village, to celebrate with his wife and small baby-daughter. We gave him one month's salary in advance, which was not very much, a suit-piece for his wife and I had sewn a nice little dress for his baby. Of course, we never saw him again, and we found out, that he had neither wife, nor child. This was lesson No 1 for me.

My first summer, we spent back in Lahore with my in-laws. We got 2 rooms on the lower storey of the house, where we had finally a bit of privacy. I started to learn the local language, Urdu, and learned about the daily chores in a Pakistani household. During the worst of summer heat I met a Swiss lady who was married to an East Pakistani, a scientist in the atomic research commission. She invited me to go with her to Murree, in the hills. There the weather was much cooler, and we spent the next month there with her 2 daughters and Yasmin.

The truck business did not do well. My husband, being a very honest person, trusted everyone and was cheated royally by drivers and other employees. In winter, our trucks had to work for a sugar-mill, which was situated at Tando Mohammad Khan, a very tiny town, in the surroundings of Hyderabad. So we moved there. My husband had hired a "furnished bungalow" for us, and I was quite excited. When we reached there, I was quite shocked to find the bungalow to be a tiny house: one room, furnished with a small table and 2 chairs on one side, on the other side a "charpoy", a kind of cot, woven with strings. At night we squeezed another charpoy in, only by taking out the chairs. In front there was a veranda, where I had to do my cooking, sitting on a "piri" on a small kerosene oil stove. I could never leave the stove, for fear of the cats of the neighbours, or the chicken my husband insisted to keep on the roof. The courtyard was small, with one tree, giving a bit of shade. In Sindh it is hot even in winter. Near the door there were the usual 2 cubicles, one for ablutions, the other served as toilet. Every morning the sweepress came to wash out the refuse into a small open gutter, passing in front of all the houses. One day Yasmin slipped and fell into that filth and I had to give her a bath with cold water, as there was no time to heat some on the stove, she was so dirty! To take a bath, there was hardly enough space in the "bathroom" to squeeze in a bucket with water. Therefore my husband always did his ablutions outside in the courtyard, wearing a loincloth (dhoti). This was of course not allowed to a woman. There was no running water, and the "Mashiqi"- or waterman brought the water, carrying it in a huge leather-pouch, on his back, filling a drum with a small faucet.

Well, this was practically my first own home in Pakistan, and I was quite happy. My immediate neighbours came once to introduce themselves, but as there was the language problem, we did not see each other again. We lived in this "bungalow" for a bit more then 4 months, and only once did we go to Karachi to meet some relatives of mine, who passed by ship on a cruise to India. When I explained where we lived, they said politely, "Your house seems to be quite primitive", and only then did I realize how very primitive we were living.

Now, being on my own I wanted to finish with the cave-age laundry. Therefore I bought some washing powder. But unfortunately that was so strong, that the skin of my hands got very much affected, and bleeding, so no more washing for me. That was the time, to hire another boy for me. He was quite friendly, but of course spoke only Sindhi and a very few words of Urdu. He also played with Yasmin, which resulted in her learning the local language, and absolutely refusing to understand anything I said in English. I being a fool, let her do so, and as I had to learn the language also, started speaking with her in Urdu which I picked up slowly from my husband, so we both learned her "mother-tongue" side by side.

As a woman, I could of course not do any shopping. The groceries were bought by our servant. I used to give him small amounts to pay for the vegetables and other small necessities. One day Afzal passed through the market and was accosted by several merchants, asking him to pay for all the things we had borrowed!! Of course these people are desperately poor, and the temptation to help themselves to a bit of money from their "rich" masters was too big. After this, Afzal did his shopping himself!!

Yasmin spent a lot of time with Rashid (I believe that was his name). So, not surprisingly she also caught lice from him. The day I found out, I cried, not knowing that I was also affected; something unheard of in those times here in Switzerland. Being practically locked in for months, eaten alive by mosquitoes every night, I was very much homesick. I fear my poor little Yasmin had to bear the brunt of my ill-health and frustration.

How happy I was when by April we were moving to a simple, but new flat in Hyderabad. What a luxury! We had running water, a shower and finally we got our fridge. I was in heaven, high time also, as I was highly pregnant with Samina by that time.

Hyderabad

If I remember correctly we moved to Hyderabad in April. After Tando, he flat we lived in was heaven. Two big rooms, a store, a bathroom with a shower and running water!! And even a separate kitchen, all of course very simple and rudimentary. But we were alone, and we could go out. On some weekends we went for picnics to a nearby dam, a few times even to the cinema, where they showed American pictures. We did not own a car at the time, so these outings were by Tonga, an open horse-drawn carriage, and we always had children running after us and calling" Mehm sahib, Mehm sahib". This was too much for Afzal, and the outings became rare. Finally I decided to sew myself a "burqa", a kind of sleeveless coat, with a scarf, covering the head, and also the face. So we could go out without being stared at.

In June Samina was born in a missionary hospital. I had a very bad time because I was weak from the heat and illness. In those days one stayed in hospital after the delivery for 7 days, and I enjoyed my stay very much. It was just like a holiday. On my return Azra had come to help me with the household and the baby. She did mostly the cooking and crockery, the rest I did myself. This was also the time we received visits from family members. In Pakistan it was custom to visit family for holidays, mostly the mothers with the children, quite unannounced and staying for a few days or even weeks. As people traveled with their bedrolls, there was no excuse of lack of bedding or space. This was quite normal, and only my European upbringing made me feel uneasy. My father in law had also promised to visit us, but as I bore no grandson, he postponed his visit.

I remember my very first invitation with horror: Afzal invited his cousin with family for lunch. So I cooked as best I could on the primitive stove, some kind of roast, with vegetables and potatoes. The unusual food disappeared in minutes, and everyone waited for the un-existing main course. What horror. I was so embarrassed! After this I did my best to learn the Pakistani way of cooking, with a choice of a few different curries and lots of rice.

The summer in Hyderabad was terribly hot, and my girls and I got more and more sick. Malaria had weakened me down to the bones. The girls also were very thin and always suffering from fever or loose motions. So when I sent a photo to my mother, she invited me to return for a holiday, promising me to pay my airfare. An invitation I hurried to accept, as I was terribly homesick.

The trucking business had run out, nothing was left, all the money we had brought from UK gone, and once more we stood at a crossroad. What to do and where to go. To do business in Pakistan one has to be very crafty and vigilant. Too common are the traps and the dishonesty of employees and customers. I believe this is not much different in the West, but here at least there is the law, which is widely ignored in the East.

That was the time when Afzal met the ex-manager of the business, who turned out not to be dishonest, only careless. He saw how hard Afzal worked, and offered him a working partnership in a business in Faisalabad. So while I went for 3 months to Switzerland, Afzal shifted to Faisalabad, which then was still named Lyallpur.

How I enjoyed my stay with my mother. I could go out whenever I wished, and wherever I wanted. The climate was good and the 3 of us recovered from the hot and often humid climate of Pakistan. My daughters became nice and round again, and my nerves were back to normal.

I returned in July, in time for the 3rd birthday of Yasmin, to a new start.

Lyallpur

After my stay in Switzerland for 3 months I returned happily to Pakistan. My health and the health of my daughters had improved a lot, and I was full of good intentions and plans for the future. I was also 6 months pregnant.

Faisalabad, which was then still called Lyallpur, is a sprawling city of I believe a few million inhabitants. But it is an entirely commercial city, no culture. There is of course the university, but for the common people there is nothing. There are huge parks, but at that time for women there was only the small "lady-baag". With the time of course it has improved, and now one can see ladies everywhere. I always said that Lyallpur was the biggest village on earth.

Afzal had rented the lower portion of a house with 4 rooms. The yard had a small strip of earth, where I could plant a few flowers. There was also a hand pump, because the water was only flowing twice daily for an hour. There was a water-tank of course, but as we shared it with the people who lived in the upstairs flat, it was often empty. Afzal also surprised me with some furniture; finally we had proper beds, a big improvement from the flat in Hyderabad. The girls were very happy to be back with their father, especially Samina, who had difficulties to adjust in Switzerland.

Hardly a month passed and I had a new attack of Malaria-fever. This time it was worse, and the advanced pregnancy did not help. I had to take very strong medicines, which made me worry for the health of by unborn baby for the rest of my pregnancy. Prenatal care in Pakistan at the time consisted in a monthly check-up, some extra vitamins, and that was it. Ultrasound was not available yet, so there was no proper check on the unborn baby's health. Well, all was fine after all, and better, it was a boy. Quite a scraggy baby, due to my illness I believe, but to his father he was the most beautiful baby he had ever seen.

This time the family came visiting: the grandfather, grandmother and the aunts. We celebrated the "Hakkikah", offered 2 goats prescribed in Islam for the birth of a boy. 1/3 was given to the poors, 1/3 was distributed to the neighbours, the rest went into a feast for the relatives.

By this time I was quite accustomed to the Pakistani way of life: The Kerosene stove, on the floor, where I did my cooking, sitting on a "Piri", a small stool. I had learned to make the chapattis, the parathas and to cook curries, Pilaws and local sweet-dishes. Clothes were still washed by hand, but I had most of the time some kind of household help.

As we slept outside in summer, I also knew how to tighten the strings of the woven "charpoys", which were covered with thin mattresses and had to be stood next to the wall every morning .The rooms were too hot to spend the nights. So everyone slept in the courtyard, with a fan to move the hot air a bit, allowing an un-restful sleep. No need to say, that the first rays of sun, as early as 6 o'clock woke everyone. The worst season for me was the monsoon. People and beast awaited the rain with impatience. Sometimes it poured, and brought a much awaited respite from the heat. Children were in the streets to play, enjoying the downpour, as the rain was warm. But when it stopped raining, the air became humid, and although it was less hot, the humidity made life miserable. But, of course, the mosquitoes enjoyed it, and descended on us poor humans in swarms. The kids also got fever regularly, and so did I. Sleeping outside became impossible, and the rooms were like ovens, in spite of the fans, which tried in vain to give a bit of respite.

Afzal was now working as a contractor for the government to build roads. The work was mostly done by hand, there was not much machinery apart from old fashioned road-rollers, but I am always surprised, how comparably well these simple roads last. He was very often away for a few days, and I was a bit uneasy, especially towards the end of my pregnancy. Not to be so alone, we called Azra to stay with me. My girls were delighted. Azra was a very good story-teller, quite contrary to me, and they loved her and her endless stories very much.

Wars

Soon, after Shahid's birth in 1965, the situation between India and Pakistan detoriated. One morning, I do not recall in which month, Afzal told me, that Indian forces had entered Pakistan and were marching towards Lahore. There had also been some bombing during the night. Therefore he left with his partner, Mr. Bari, to go and bring his parents to our home. We thought that Faisalabad, as Lyallpur was now called, was safer than Lahore. They left early morning in a car, and nobody knew what would come next. I was waiting the whole morning, very much worried. In the early afternoon a Rickshaw stopped before our house. There was Rashida with her boys and Azra, Ammi-jan was also there, but not my husband. At their sight I broke out in tears. The road to Lahore being 2 to 2 1/2 hours drive, I could not understand why the family had not met him and feared the worst, so I cried. This was a bad mistake, as the family thought, that I cried because I had so many visitors. That was of course not the case. By and bye I was told, that they had been at the railway-station since early morning. There were not enough trains and buses to accommodate everyone who wanted to flee the city. Also bahu-jee refused to leave his home. Some hours later Afzal reached with his father, totally exhausted, because all the roads were blocked, and the drive lasted for hours.

Well, all is well, that ends well. Life went on as usual. Afzal went to his work in the nearby villages, and Azra and I kept the house running. No need to say, that the servant boy left for his village also, so all the household chores had to be done by ourselves. There was very strict black-out at night. Often there was bombing-alarm, but actually only a few bombs were dropped on our airport, which then was very small and unimportant. I remember, the first few times there was an alarm, Afzal made us all lie on the floor. But of course we soon refused such exaggerated behaviour. Exaggeration was the norm those days. Here a small story to explain:

Afzal used to drive to his work on a Lambretta (a scooter), and often it was dark when he returned. Like in all wars, there were wardens who had to enforce the blackout, and they felt very important, and were very much over-zealous. So one evening he returned from work, with of course, the lights switched off, he was arrested by some wardens. He had forgotten to cover his back-lights! Some hot words were exchanged, and someone even accused him of being an Indian spy. But they gave him a few cuffs and let him go.

Later that evening there was a knock at the gate. It was the same warden, calling my husband out in the street. As Afzal used to imbibe a few pegs of whisky in the evenings, he went out very angry. Well, the result was that he was taken to the police-station. To drink in Pakistan was a criminal offence. So no need to say, that I was horrified. I did not sleep a wink the whole night, not knowing what the morning would bring. Because of the curfew, nobody could go to inquire also. Police stations do not have a very good reputation in Pakistan, and anything could have happened. I must say, that during that whole, long night, none of Afzal's relatives stood by me to console me, quite on the contrary, they blamed me for his drinking---was I not the infidel European with the loose morals (like all western ladies!!!). I have had plenty of misunderstandings with my in-laws, and quite often it was my fault, and lack of understanding of each others culture and customs. But this night I could never forget or forgive. Early morning Afzal returned, telling us, that at the police station they gave him a charpoy, and released him as soon as the curfew was lifted.

The war only lasted a few weeks; I think the UN ordered a cease-fire. There was not too much damage done, everyone returned to their homes, servants returned to their work and life continued like before. But we soon left this house and shifted to a different part of the city.

There was another short war over Kashmir in 1971. Khalida and her kids came to stay with us, because the army evacuated their home, which was very near the border. This time everyone was calm, no more hysteria. I can't even remember, if there were black-outs at night, probably yes, but I don't remember. All I can remember, that Khalida came with an awful lot of food-stuff, which lasted us for long after she had returned to her home.

About Dacoits And Highwayrobbers

After the war Afzal returned to his job, building roads. One of the roads he was working on passed through a village which was famous for harbouring a family of dacoits. It was said, that they kidnapped children and sold them to beggars. They also were involved in lots of robberies, and there was a time, when it was not safe to pass through their village after sunset.

Now, what happened, that these few brothers approached my husband with some demand for money, to let him progress through their village. Afzal must have refused, so a proper fight between the villagers and the road-workers began. Some of the men were quite badly injured. With the help of his employees Afzal managed to get hold of one of the "famous" brothers. He tied him up, put him in the car and dropped him at the police station, not before being threatened, that they will abduct his family.

At that time we were living in a 4-room house with a huge garden around it. I was very pleased, as there were lots of roses, and even a fig-tree and a banana-plant. The only problem was that the gate could not be properly fixed. No need to tell, that the warning did not fall on closed ears. We had 3 children, the smallest; Shahid was nearly a year old. To help us out, one of our employees gave us his guard dog, a huge brute, which made me afraid also. But, of course, the moment we let him loose, he ran back to his master, although he was living at the other end of town.

Because we took the warning quite serious, there was nothing else to do, but shift our home. The one we were living in was known to some men of that village who worked for Afzal on the road.

There was quiet for months, and we did not hear anymore about that story. But one evening, someone rang our doorbell. Yasmin answered to a man who inquired about her father. Luckily he had not yet returned from work, because we saw through the window, that there were 5 or 6 men in a Tonga (horse-cart), all with rifles. They waited for some time, and then left, before my husband returned. After all, I believe that they just wanted to frighten us, in which they succeeded.

Another, similar incident happened later somewhere else. Again there was the road to be built. During the days truckloads of stones, to be used in the work were delivered, but regularly, during the night they disappeared again. So Afzal and his first worker stayed up one night and caught the thieves red-handed. Again there was a fight. The poor employee had some serious head-wounds, but the robbers managed to take him and my husband to their village, were they kept them. Some of the workers informed Afzal's partner, who quickly drove to the site of the fight. I do not remember how the affair ended, whether some money was paid, or the police had to intervene. But as I got my husband back a day later, I can only say, all is well that ends well

About Cars And Accidents

We bought our first car when Yasmin started going to college. As we were always living at the edge of town, the English Missionary- School was quite far away. So my poor children had to get the school bus the first, and were dropped the last, which made 3 hours to go and come. With all the homework they got, there was very little time to play and relax. But nasty time went on; our financial situation became better also. From the road-building-business we went on to become working-partner in a small factory with Mr. Bari. Afzal was too honest, which did not please the family of Bari, as the profit was not big enough. So under pretence of Afzal's dishonesty, they threw him out. The reason was that my mother sent me a little money, with which we bought some land, to build a small house. Our first house was built with a loan of 40'000 Rs, which at the time was around 10,000 Swiss Francs. It was a very simple house with 4 rooms, kitchen and 2 toilets.

Later we became partners with Masooda's husband, who at the time lived in East Pakistan, which is now Bangladesh. Again all went well, till they had to leave Bangladesh, and the sons wanted to take over the business. Again he was accused of being dishonest, and he left under protest. I find it strange, that all they could find was his dishonesty, because he was very hard-working. He was also meticulously honest. I remember how he made me pay even for the useless old cotton bags, which I gave sometimes to my servants, and for which they could find some use. But as he was so honest, he believed in others, and he was very often cheated by his employees.

Only when we changed partners once more could we

finally afford a car. It was a second-hand Suzuki-van. Therefore, at over 40, I had to learn driving. I was horrified of the uncontrolled Faisalabad traffic, and did not well at all, till one day my husband said:" Yes, I believe you are right, you will never learn to drive", that was after I had parked the car no near a pillar in our house, that it was impossible to drive it either way, and we had to lift it. After hearing this, my pride was hurt, so from next day I managed to drive. I never had an accident, the worst that happened, was when I backed into a lamp-post. Yasmin also learned driving very quickly, and drove accident-free.

Not so Afzal. He hated driving a car, and much preferred his Lambretta. He was also a terrible driver. When Yasmin had her first baby, Salim was in Saudi Arabia. So, after he left, we intended to drive to Lahore to collect her and Jiha, to spend some time with us. Luckily we left the children at home. Outside the town Afzal insisted to drive, and I was also scared, the roads being narrow and dangerous. So that day, a nice and sunny day in Oct or Nov., we drove along in a good mood, looking forward to our first grandchild. Afzal had the bad habit of turning his face to speak, even while driving, and with it he always turned the steering wheel a bit. Well this time all went wrong: The road was elevated and narrow at that place, so by turning, he lost control, and the car fell down the slope, overturning at least once. A young couple who came from the opposite side helped us out of the wreck and took us to a nearby hospital. After first-aid Afzal insisted to return to his car. We were very near Lahore, but he wanted to drive the wreck back to Faisalabad. The roof was caved in, all the windows were broken, and there was no windshield. The door could not be closed, so we tied it with my dubutta! But the engine was running. Afzal had 2 broken ribs, I had crushed vertebrae, and both of us were blue and bruised all over. It was an ordeal to turn to see if nobody was behind, as the back-mirror was also gone, and he had to go slow. But we drove home, exciting a lot of stares on the way. At a petrol-pump someone offered to drive us home, as the car was not worth saving, but Afzal refused.

In Faisalabad, we drove through the middle of a wedding-crowd. I still remember their faces while looking at us. The children of course were horrified also to see us arrive in this way. Well, we survived obviously, and I suppose that is the most important fact!!

The police did not have to be called, because no other vehicle was involved. Also, there is not much of an ambulance service, as

I had to find out 20 years later, when we had another accident, this time involving a tree. But this time Afzal did not survive.

Another Funny Story Or Two

I remember another story, which we can laugh about now.

Afzal's eldest brother, Saeed was a major in the army. He had fallen in love with a married woman, and later married her. Nobody in the family accepted his wife as a proper daughter-in-law, although she tried her best to please. Maybe this was a reason, that they were always very nice to us, and understanding us. Saeed kept inviting us to his house, but my husband did not believe in visiting relatives more than necessary.

On a family-wedding in Lahore, we all met. We were then already living in Faisalabad, and had 3 children. Once more the nice brother-in-law insisted on our visiting him, why not now, he said. So all of a sudden Afzal agreed. He thought we could travel with Saeed and his family by car, and return a few days later by train. Now Saeed could not refuse. They were already 2 grown-ups and 3 children in their small car. But he managed to pile us in too---a total of 3 adults and 6 kids! The drive between Lahore and Rawalpindi, where he was stationed at the time was a minimum of 5 hours, as there were no auto routes yet. I remember that some of the children were sitting on the floor between the seats. I am quite sure, the trip was not very enjoyable, and Saeed was not really in a good mood. When we reached Rawalpindi, everyone looked for the house-keys. They were nowhere to be found. Until finally the elder son, who must have been between 10 and 12, remembered, that he had put them on the car-roof just before we left! So we drove to the canteen, to wait for someone to break the locks.

But my children, who had never had a holiday, enjoyed our

stay very much. And I must say, Saeed and his wife were graceful hosts, and never let me feel the awkwardness of the situation.

One more, small tale:

For a long time, we did not possess a car. Afzal used a Vespa for his work, and this became also the family-vehicle. It was seldom, that we traveled with one kid standing in front, one sitting between the two of us and me in lady-seat fashion, with a baby on my lap; all this, with the dubutta flapping in the wind. This is not at all unusual in Pakistan. I even went to the hospital for the delivery of one of my kids on the Vespa.

Once we had to take a puppy to the vet. He was sitting on my lap, and yapping all the way to the hospital, and I kept laughing. With everyone staring, my husband was not very pleased.

And another one:

Faisalabad was created by an Englishman by the name of Lyall (Therefore the old name of Lyallpur). The commercial centre has a monument in the middle and from there 7 streets part in every direction in the form of a star. Each street has its own business, more or less. In one you will find mostly cloth-stores, in another bookstores and all that has to do with writing, in a third fruit and vegetables, yet in another spices, and big pieces of rock salt, which some house wives still prefer to the packed, refined salt common everywhere now. I also have a mortar and pestle for grinding salt and spices before I bought myself an electric grinder.

These roads and bazaars are always very crowded, apart from pedestrians, who walk in the middle of the road; there are donkey carts, camel carts, cars and lots of scooter-rickshaws. My husband never ventured with his car into the middle of this teeming crowd; but I had learned to crawl through the masses to reach as near as possible to my chosen destination. One day, as I tried to leave the center by the usual route through the spices-bazaar, the traffic seemed to be worse, and all in the opposite direction. When I reached, at walking speed, the other end of the road, a policeman stopped me, to tell me, that this was a one-way road. So what to do now? He was very casual about it, and let me go, with a warning to be more careful another time! This is not so unusual, as traffic signs are sometimes hidden behind a bush or the advertisement for a shop; also, they kept changing the routes, trying in vain to control the impossible chaos. Well, all is well that ends well!

This kind of travel-system did never seem odd to me. Sometimes I am astonished how easy I found it, to accept a totally different life from my earlier one. Not everything was easy of course, but I never tried to change something, or demanded some more comfort. I just tried to make the Best of the situation. Maybe I was wrong, but the times changed for the Better anyhow.

Entertainement

At the end I would like to write a few words also about the enjoyments I and my children had. Of course there were then no amusement parks. We also did not have Television for quite some time. But in the evenings we used to play Monopoly or Scrabble or other games. There is a very nice zoo in Lahore, so on every visit to Lahore, where all our relatives lived, we visited the zoo.

But the real funs were the pick nicks. Sometimes in summer, especially when we had visitors, we borrowed a car and went out of the town for a pick nick. We searched for a secluded spot, near a canal or other waterway. There we could planch to our hearts content, without being seen, but nevertheless wholly dressed, the children of course in underwear, as they had no swimming-costumes. That was really fun.

Other enjoyments were the weddings. On weddings all the neighbours are always invited, so these occasions were quite frequent. In the evening before the "Rukhsati" the young girls get together to dance and sing. There are competitions between the party of the bride and that of the bridegroom, to make fun in their songs of the relatives of the opposite group.

Also there were the visits of the cousins of my kids, which for them was also very nice.

All in all, I believe my kids had a simple but not unhappy childhood. Of course their expectations were not as high as are the children's of today.

My "Servants"

I have often been told, that I had an easy life, as I always had servants to help me with the household chores. Well yes, that is true in a way. I mostly had a woman who came every day for the cleaning -- sweeping the house with a "jaroo" --- a bundle of reed, and washing the floors with a damp cloth. Dusting was left to me, and mind you, in a country where it does not rain for months, there is plenty of dust. Also from time to time we had dust storms, when the whole house had to be washed; of course I had to help there too.

Then there is the washing: in summer one wears cotton-dresses. They often have to be starched, and of course changed every day. The children wear white uniforms to go to school which rarely last two days without washing. Before I had a washing machine, my cleaning woman used to wash as well. Later, with a simple machine which washed only, I had to do the rinsing by hand. And then there was the ironing, at least 2 to 3 times per week.

Cooking is also not an easy chore. For lunch we usually ate curry -- meat and vegetables--- with chapatti, which had to be prepared fresh for every meal. It took me quite some time to learn to knead the dough just right, and to prepare round and thin chapattis. Evening meals were mostly rice and some lentils, there is such a variety available in Pakistan.

There was also always a lot of crockery to be washed.

In the afternoon I usually spent some time sewing for my children. I loved doing it, and ready-made garments not available at the time, it saved me quite a bit of money.

Yes, most of the time I had some kind of household help. They were often young boys from villages in their early teens. Not seldom they left after having been taught the rudimentary of helping in a clean household. They did the crockery, looked after the small children, and often went to buy the daily needed items from some nearby shops. It was quite a job to try to control the thefts of small change or household items.

One boy came from a village nearby. He was very nice, liked to work and got along nicely with my children. He stayed with our family until he was old enough to go and work in a factory, maybe 3 years. When he worked and was already married he often came to visit us. On one of those visits he told me, that while bringing the milk from the milk shop nearby, he used to drink some, and refill the container with water. This was easy, as milk used to be sold open in a small bucket. He laughed when he told us the story.

Another boy stayed with us to look after the baby and do the shopping. We had an agreement to send him to school, so he could get some education, all while earning a bit of money after school. My husband got called by the teacher several times, because the boy did not learn, and eventually stopped going to school at all. When we found out, we sent him back to his parents.

At one time, when I was already working I had an old women staying with me all day long. This was more to have someone at home when the cleaning was done, and sometimes my elder children returned from college before me. It was quite safe to let the lady stay in the empty house, as she returned every afternoon to her home, empty-handed of course, as I thought. Only much later did I learn, that while I was away at work, the lady's grandchildren used to come to visit, taking with them rice, sugar, flour and cooking oil!

But this type of bother one has to learn to keep up with. I have had watches, rings, garments and money stolen.

Boys and girls from villages very often work in households. As they do not go to school in any case, their families are quite happy to have a mouth less to feed, and get some salary as well. Usually these children, some as young as 8, are really better off like this. They have enough to eat, decent clothes and they love to watch television. Most families treat them nicely, and they do not have more work to do, then they would have to at their own home. But of course there are people who mistreat them, and there is unfortunately no control over the situation.

I also am against child labor. But very often it is a case of these children working, or starving. Children in households are better off then others who have to work in factories, brick kilns or carpet weaving shops. As I worked for a short time in a garment export factory, I was shocked by the hypocrisy of the buyers, who haggled over every penny, at the same time as forbidding child labor. Maybe if they had paid a little bit more, the fathers could be better paid, and children did not have to work!

Visitors

Mama

I think it was in the year 1969 or 70, in December, when my mother came to visit me for the first time. She came by boat, landing at Karachi, where we went to receive her. For me it was like birthday and Christmas together. I missed my mother very much, and only now, that I am far away from my daughters and grandchildren, do I realize, how lonely she must have felt at the time.

Mama adjusted to our more or less primitive kind of living like a fish taking to water. She found our Shalwar-Kamise* very comfortable, and after a little time wore only that, which suited her very much. She looked a bit like a smart Pakistani lady. The food was also no problem for her, as she liked eating spicy.

Unfortunately, a few days after her arrival, on the very day we wanted to travel to Lahore, to meet Afzal's parents, his father died, quite unexpectedly. So we left anyhow, and mama had the experience to assist at the funeral customs. But I will tell about that in some other chapter.

I think that mama came with an open ticket for her return. As summer approached, I was getting worried because of the heat. At that time, we did not have any air-conditioning. This kind of luxury was very rare at the time, and mostly only to find in 4 or 5- star hotels or restaurants, which were out of reach for us anyhow. But my mother seemed to stand the heat better than myself, and she said that she enjoyed sleeping on the roof, under the stars with us. So summer passed and the Monsoon season started. Now I was getting real anxious and asked her, if she did not want to return.

But she seemed to be happy with us, and quite healthy, apart from having lost some weight.

But things can not always go well. Not surprisingly, she got malaria-fever. After the treatment she had grown very weak. In this state of health she attended the marriage of my youngest sister-in-law, Azra. It must have been quite a stress for her.

Meaning well, Afzal and I decided to send her for a few weeks to Murree, in the hills, where the climate was cooler, so that she could recuperate.

Murree is a tourist village in the hills, quite near the capital, where Pakistanis go for holidays during the summer holidays. It has beautiful forests and view on the mountains, the Karakorums, or pre-Himalayas. I believed, that 2 weeks in the cool and green nature would do her good. Of course, the kind of « hotel » we could afford was very simple. Any establishment where travelers can sleep, is called hotel. There are even some who hire out charpoys* to be put up in the street to pass the night. But there of course, she did have a room to herself, if only a very plain one.

She was back in a week's time, telling us, that she felt too lonely there, not being able to talk to anybody. But after her return she left soon. I think that she had to be treated for some kind of tropical decease after her return to Switzerland, but she never told me.

Mama came to visit twice more, but for a shorter period, and the last time, in 1975, I believe, she was not feeling well, had problems with the food, and stayed in bed quite often.

Margaret

I have always tried to keep contact with my family in Switzerland, and wrote as much as possible. So, in one of my letters to my cousin, Margaret, I invited her to visit me. When she accepted, I was at first overjoyed. Margaret was not only my cousin, but we were best friends and went to school together. But after the first excitement passed, I got a bit scared. It was 1989; we had just sold a house which was over our budget, intending to build a more reasonable one, and shifted to a rented one. The house was simple, with 3 bedrooms, and quite nicely built. The problem was that before us it had been lived in by several families, and it was in a terrible state of hygiene! This was nothing new to me. I was used, after every shifting to rented houses, to first make war on cockroaches, and clean thoroughly. But would my cousin, who was living in a lovely Swiss house, be able to adjust? And what about the food? Pakistani everyday food does not have much variety. How should I cook, and keep her healthy for the 2 weeks (or was it 3) she was spending with me? I got quite nervous.

But I need not have worried. Margaret seemed to adjust quite well.

By this time, we had a car and I was driving inside the city. So our outings to the bazaars were easier to manage. What I did not realize at the time, that all these trips in and outside the city were very stressful for my poor cousin. I had of course long got used to the chaos in Pakistan's traffic, but for her, as she told me later, it was nerve-wrecking.

We tried to show her a bit of our country. We visited Lahore, the big Badshahi mosque, the Fort and Shalimar garden. Probably also the zoo, and were invited to all our relative's homes.

Yasmin and Samina were already married by that time, and Salim served us as guide to the historical places. He knows history quite well, and with him, the visits became more worthwhile.

The crowning of Margaret's visit was to be a short tour to the Northern valleys. My dear husband did not want to accompany us, so I was left on my own. As we had never really traveled before, I had no idea how to organize the trip, but I wrongly hoped the tourist offices would be able to help me. But in November, the tourist season was over, and I had practically no help. If I asked for a reasonably priced hotel in Islamabad, I was advised the 4 or 5-star hotels with European prices, which for us « Pakistanis » was just not affordable. So we had some interesting experiences:

Firstly we traveled to Rawalpindi by train, in the sleeper-compartment, which we shared with two more ladies. Sleepers are equipped with 2 benches for the day, and two upper-storied perches to fold down during the night. One has to bring one's own bedding. This type of travel is not very comfortable, but as Margaret says, it was an experience!

Well, we reached Rawalpindi very early in the morning, deposited our bedding at the station and took a taxi to a small hotel, recommended by a neighbor. Arriving there, at around 5 in the morning, nobody opened the door. It was still night, and we did not know what to do. Luckily we spotted a nice place at walking distance. High time, as a man was lurking in the street, and seemed to take an unpleasant interest in us. Well, two lone ladies, and Europeans on top, in the middle of the night, or almost, were suspicious. But the hotel was quite nice, and he charged us only one night, even though we arrived so early.

Later that morning we first went to the Bazaar, and then to the PIA office, trying to book a flight for the northern valleys. But no way: There are daily flights to all the northern destinations with Fokker-planes. But, as the mountains to cross are quite high, and the planes small, these flights have to be cancelled in bad weather. So at the travel agents we were told, that there was a flight today, but as the weather was changing, they could not assure us the return flight for the next few days. So there went out plans. But we did book the return flight for Faisalabad. At the tourist office we were advised to go to Murree and from there across the mountain pass to Abbotabad. Not very original, but lets go!

In Murree again we were misled by the tourist-office and sent to a hotel which was a bit low standard. But as we only wanted to stay the night, it had to do. In Murree Margaret experienced her first snow of the season! Funny, coming from Switzerland, the first snow in Pakistan!!!

The bus-line between Murree and Abbotabad was prehistoric! A bus; which seemed to fall to pieces any minute. As passengers, apart from us, only men, a goat and some chickens. The road was badly maintained at the time, very narrow and dangerous. When a vehicle had to pass from the opposite side, our bus had to drive so near the abyss, that from the window you could see right into the nothing. We were both scared, but as Margaret told me later, she thought she was going to die, I believed, that this buses passed here everyday, and knowing that every now and then one fell down the steep slopes, I hoped that it would not happen today! Apart from that, the trip was wonderful; a beautiful view into the Himalayas or Karakorums, wonderful forests and rivers. One could think to be in the Swiss Alps.

In Abbottabad there was again the hotel-problem. First I saw a place where we deposited our luggage. We had to pay for one night in advance. It was very cheap, and very dirty as well, not a place to stay at all. Later we found a more reasonable place to spend the night.

On our return we wanted to stay the last day in Islamabad. This is the capital and is built in American fashion with straight roads in squares. There are very fashionable sections, with beautiful modern buildings, but also in the by lanes, the usual small houses for the « common people ». Well, this time we were not going to have problems with accommodation. The Swiss lady had bought a guide which recommended us to a small hotel called « Blue moon ». What horror! This was obviously a hippy-hotel, small, not very clean, and cheap. We paid, deposited our luggage and went site-seeing. On our return in the afternoon, we entered the wrong room with our key, realizing, that there was probably only one key for all the rooms. That was enough, and we found a lovely guest house to spend the last night, before our return to Faisalabad.

Liselot

In spring 1999, when Liselot, or Mona, as she likes to be called, visited me, I was more trained. I also drove the car all over the country, which gave us more freedom to go where we wanted to. Mona was very kind to invite me to stay with her in simple but nice and clean hotels, some of which she knew from an earlier visit with her partner. At the time she attended the marriage of Shahid, and I had absolutely no time to show her around.

Now, in March 1999, I was completely free, and we enjoyed a few nice weeks together. The starting point of our adventure was Lahore. Mona could not get enough of the bazaars, and we used to drive through the different quarters of the sprawling Capital of the Punjab. Lahore has lots of old Moghul monuments, like the Fort, the big Mosque and also Shalimar gardens. Then you can find very old bazaars like Anarkali, or also modern shopping centers with an Asian touch anyhow.

It was the time of the Eid* festival, where Muslims have to scarify goats. So there were goats, sheep and camels everywhere, a fact which irritates me, but somehow fascinated Mona.

After a few days in Lahore Afzal joined us, and we traveled to Mangla. It is a drive of around 4 to 5 hours, and one passes through all of Punjab, crossing 3 of the main rivers of Pakistan. Mangla is one of Asia's biggest dams. It's lake takes care of the irrigation of most of Pakistan and provides most of its electricity. This dam has been built by the Italians. They left behind a full colony of living quarters and houses, which have been taken over by the Pakistan army. The Mangla-cantonment is one of the most important, as it lays in Kashmir, quite near the disputed border with India. But the houses are in a terrible state of disarray.

As my son-in-law is an officer in the army, he was posted there at the time. He needed a special permit for the visit of a foreigner. I am of course added to his visitors-list as a relative, and not considered foreign any more.

As mentioned, the house was in a terrible state, kitchen and baths horrible. But of course it was nicely furnished and had a wonderful garden with huge very old trees. Also it was the festival of Eid. For Eid every Muslim, who can afford it has to slaughter a goat or sheep, to distribute the meat among the poor. Some people also put their money together for a cow or camel. As meat is comparatively expensive, the poor people of Pakistan sometimes get only meat during the Eid festival. I was horrified every year of the slaughtering, which was done in the backyard, even though I can see the usefulness of the exercise. Often I pleaded, that the money should be given to a poor person to buy a goat, but of course I was not heard. Mona was very brave about it, and filmed everything, to the amusement of the butchers.

After 3 days of Eid at Zarina's we continued to Islamabad. 2 days in Islamabad were enough to see mainly the modern Mosque, the shopping bazaar, where one can find lots of gold-jewelry and handicrafts for all the foreign guests and diplomats. Islamabad has a diplomatic sector for all the embassies. It is now locked by a gate, and can only be entered with a passport. Then there was no gate, and we enjoyed looking at the huge, modern embassy buildings.

Our next destination was Peshawar. Peshawar is the capital of the North-West province. There live the rustic Pathans. In this province one sees still more veiled women. There are also lots of Afghan refugees living there. I did not like Peshawar. I must say, its very old, famous « kissa-kahani » bazaar is interesting. Kissa-kahani means story telling. I believe, as it was on a very important road, the travelers must have stopped in Peshawar bazaar to tell their stories. And what stories that must have been, of places far away, and dangerous travels!

I would have liked to travel on a famous train to the border with Afghanistan, which then was still quite safe, but Mona thought it was too dangerous. On the way we also visited the ruins of Taxila, an antique site of Buddhist temples, where we also watched a match of tent-pegging. At great speed, riders on beautiful, fiery horses try to pick up a small bit of wood with a lance. It was a beautiful spectacle, and the riders are very expert. We were of course the only women, but being Europeans, were tolerated!

I must say, it was not quite « correct » for two ladies, to travel without men in this part of Pakistan. But we enjoyed the trip.

After our return to Islamabad, I let her return to Lahore by air and stayed on with my daughter for some time.

Some Letters Written To My Friend

14.1.1968

« ..... Lyallpur is the industrial center of Pakistan, a huge city but nevertheless provincial. There are no hotels of European standard, no tea-rooms, where an unveiled woman would dare to go; of course no night-club or dancing, only seldom good English films. The reason is, that Lahore lays 2 hours drive away. Therefore, the rich and mighty travel there to amuse themselves. People of « our standard » don't go out with their wives, which condemns me to be a housewife only.... »

Well, this description was accurate, but not quite true. There were the clubs, in British fashion. Here was one club, where mostly business-men went to play cards, but there was also a club for government functionaries and businessmen. In these clubs there were parties for families, they also showed good pictures regularly. To join this club would even have been good for Afzal's business, because like everywhere to have good connections helps. But he did not want to join .In his opinion, making contacts through a European wife (as he saw it) had something dishonest about it! But he being well educated and well behaved, did really not need my help to get to know people.

« ....Afzal works now as contractor for road-building, and he earns quite well, considering circumstances. I have around 1000 Rs household money - a clerk earns around 125 to 250. In spite of this my mother thought we were living very primitively. Later she saw what it means to be poor, and she left quite satisfied….. »

« ……for a European it would be a necessity to own a car, because people stare so much. Our firm possesses a Mercedes, but this is never available for me…. »

That famous Mercedes was actually the car of our main partner. But for tax-purpose, it was put in the name of the firm. There was also a driver, paid by the business. We did sometimes get it, to go to Lahore, but seldom.

« ……… my children were of course very happy to receive your parcel, good toys are not available here, or if available, very expensive…… »

Yes, in those days there was not much available, but nowadays you can get almost everything. For my son it was an ardent wish to possess a « dinky-car » once. But I don't think the children were less happy then they are now, when they have rooms full of toys.

« ……it is possible that you have to wait longer for an answer to your letter, because in a month's time it will be so hot, that the tongue hangs out - or nearly………otherwise it is ok here, to be compared with the life in an hut, where there is no comfort, but where one is feeling good anyhow…..Afzal has turned out to be a good husband and a very loving father. But the business leaves him little time for the family…………..money here is very important, more so than in Europe….. »

Yes, in Pakistan it is very important to be well-off, to be socially accepted. There is much more class difference than here. Also there is no social system, no old age pension, no sickness insurance. Our marriage also was quite ok till then. Maybe it was the frustration of continuous failures which put the worm in our relationship.

31.12.1969

« ....has my mother told you, that business is not so good at the moment? Yes, we had big losses last year, but we still have enough to live. As for holidays: Holidays as we know in Europe exist here only for the high-society. The few cooler holiday-resorts are too expensive, around 100 Rs per night (100 Rs are around 95 Fr.)............what we could do, hire an apartment for 2 weeks, but a women with children could only do that by taking at least the mother-in-law with her....... Here women go to their relatives for a few days to take holidays, but as mine are so far off, this is also no option. What I need is a hobby. Unfortunately there is no change here--once per moth to the bazaar,-- four times or less per year to see a film, --once to Lahore with the children. Otherwise nothing but household and kids. At the moment 3 of 4 have a fever and cold....... »

That was my generation, now my children go for holidays regularly. Also the inflation is such, that now 100 Rs is around 2 Fr., not 95 ,and our household expenditure came to over 25000 Rs, just for my husband and me.

31.1.1970

« .....here even the hardest winter is difficult to support. January and February are fine. During the day you sit outside in the sun whenever possible, but in the evenings you nearly die from cold. The houses are of course built for the hot season, --all stone floors und very high ceilings, absolutely impossible to heat. And more so the rainy days in winter. One wears the coat all day long, or sits inside the quilt , and one feels sorry for the kids who have to go to school. But luckily it rains only for a few days each winter.... »

The most one could do against the cold, was to sit around a small coal-stove, which let off some horrible fumes. Later, when we had natural gas, there were gas-ovens in every room. Also, with air-conditioning the ceilings are less high now. Then came also the wall to wall carpet fashion; very inappropriate with all the dust there is, but less cold in winter.

« ....my youngest does not leave me one free minute. Here babies are not allowed to cry, therefore they become quite tyrannical. Almost the whole day they are carried around or play with them. This type of baby-care has been thought to me by my mother-in-law. So I employ a 12 year old girl, who washes my crockery and entertains the baby. I am then the whole day busy with sewing, ironing, cooking and mending,,,..... Almost everyday some neighbors come for tea or to inquire about a sick child, wasting a lot of ones time...... »

T0 End

There are of course many more stories of how we have lived; the children's school, their marriages, and my job later. Also I could have talked of my children, about my grandchildren etc. But I only wanted to show here the difference between 1961, when we shifted to Pakistan, and the end nineties. In these nearly 40 years we changed from a single room house with a small kerosene stove, no running water, and no proper toilet to a modern house with 3 or even 4 bedrooms, attached bathrooms; running hot and cold water, bathtubs, Ac's, gas heaters in winter, Microwave oven, washing machine and all other household machines. But these not always easy times taught me to appreciate what I got. Every new gadget was luxury for me. And I learned to be grateful. Here in the West, people do not appreciate all the good they have, nice homes, plenty variety of foods, lovely clothes. They are never satisfied, and always crave for more. Maybe it would be helpful, if all young people should spend a year in some third-world country.

Of course there were times when I was at the very end of my tether, and feeling very unhappy, especially after one of my un-ending sicknesses. I never got adjusted to the heat and it was mostly my poor children who had to suffer from my bad moods. But my love to my husband at first, and later for my children kept me up. My education had also taught me to finish something once started. But I must admit, had it not been for my children, I might have run away several times. Also I had converted to Islam, because I believe that it is the perfect way of life; Afzal never asked me to change my religion.

If with all this effort I have learned to be satisfied with what I have, and not always wanting more, and also to feel for the people who have less, and try to help some of them, it was worth it.

I am also very proud of all my children, who have each in his or her field excelled. Whether it is in their professional life, or as wives and mothers, they are doing well, and what more could a mother wish for!

Bibliography

Baagh - garden

Baratthe - bridegroom with his guests

Burkhathe - traditional Islamic veil

Charpoys - string-cot

Dhoti - loincloth

Eid - muslim festivals

Ghara - earthen water pitcher

Handi - earthern cooking vessel

Mashiqiwaterman - a profession which does not exist anymore, as far as I know
Piria - low woven stool

Rukhsat - ceremony where the bride leaves the house of her parents

Shalwar/Kamise - Pakistani dress, consisting of wide trousers and a long shirt

Shehenai - trumpet-like instrument played at weddings

The daily life in a Middle class Pakistani family

The days start very early in a Muslim home. Even not everybody says the prayers regularly, the days are built around the Muslim practices. Morning prayer is before the sun-rise. From all the Minarets the call for prayer is heard at the time. Although the call « Allah-o-Akbar » - Allah is great- can sound very beautiful,- when it is heard from several mosques at the same time, in different styles, the beauty of it is lost.

After the morning shower, a must at least in summer, breakfast is prepared. First the dough has to be prepared to make the parathas, a kind of bread, baked on an iron skillet with butter. This is eaten with eggs or a bit of vegetable curry left over from the evening before. But English type bread is also available with bread and butter for those who prefer a lighter meal. With it one drinks tea, really strong tea with lots of milk, or in summer « Lassi » a yoghurt-drink which really cools you. My son-in-law who served under the blue helmets in Mogadishu told us that the American soldiers used to come to their compound to ask for a« Pakistani beer ».

When the children have left for school and the husband for work, usually a bit after 7 am, the whole house has to be swept and wiped with a wet cloth. This is mostly done by a cleaning woman, the daily dusting is left to the housewife. Floors are of marble tiles or cemented, polished to a nice shine. This keeps the house a bit cooler in summer, but unfortunately also in winter. Wall to wall carpets have luckily now gone out of fashion. They were totally unsuitable, because of the dust and the hot weather. But people like to have some nice rugs.

Washing also used to be done every day by hand. With the heat and the dust it is essential to change every day. Clothes are usually in cotton or some kind of artificial material. The voiles for summer need to be starched. Washing machines have only been introduced maybe in the nineties, but they are simple machines which wash and wring only. The rinsing has to be done by hand. Then the ironing is left. As you can see, household chores are much more, and some kind of servant is really necessary.

The meat used to be bought fresh every morning before we got a big fridge with a freezing compartment, then once a week was enough. For the vegetables a « rehri », a man with a small wooden cart comes every morning with fresh vegetables. Nobody would buy leftovers from the previous day. Imported fruits and vegetables have only recently come on the market. This of course hampers the variety of meals, but it is sure more healthy.

For groceries there are lots of small shops, more like stalls without doors, where all essentials can be bought. But there are convenience stores also now, more and more shopping centers are being constructed.

Kids return from school around 2 o'clock. After lunch there is a siesta. In summer mostly people sleep for an hour or two, as days beginning before 6, end around 11 at night. After the siesta homework has to be done and supervised.

I used to sew a lot for my children. Some years ago there were practically no ready made shops. But within the last 20 years this has changed drastically. Children's clothes are bought ready-made. Ladies still have their clothes mostly stitched by tailors. Men's suits for better occasions also are sewn by tailors. Of course this is not as expensive as here, as it is common practice.

Late afternoon is the time for visits. Often neighboring ladies come for a cup of tea and a chat. Some are nice, some are gossips. When visiting time is over, it is time to cook again.

Evenings are for watching TV, or playing family games. 8 o'clock for the little ones, 9 for the elders was bedtime. Once the girls went to college the times were of course not so restricted as they also needed to study.

So I had finally a bit of time for myself, reading or watching TV, of course also to discuss my problems and my husband's.

Families visit also, for a meal or just to see each other.

But my husband was very unsocial, so we stayed at home unless there was a wedding somewhere in the neighborhood presenting a welcome change for women and kids.

Let me here say something about condition of women in Pakistan. I have almost always lived in the Punjab, which is the most educated province of Pakistan. Here, in educated families the ladies have all the rights. Mostly it is them who decide anything inside the home. If they are suffering, it is more likely by the hand of a mother-in-law then by the husband. Naturally it is the women who have to adjust to the habits of the husband's family, as she belongs into this new family, having left hers by the marriage. More and more young ladies work as well now, there are lots of female doctors, teachers but also now office workers, bank managers, lawyers and judges.

The famous four wives for Muslims are also outlawed in Pakistan, unless the first wife signs a permission and there is a valid reason. For example if the woman can not have children. So, if permission is granted for a second marriage, at least the first wife has a place to live and is cared for. But this happens seldom now. Men who want a change have an affair, like everywhere else.

The situation is entirely different in the provinces of Sindh, Balochistan and the Northern areas. In the rural parts, not in the big cities, of these provinces strict « Purdah » (i.e. veil and total isolation of women) exists still. Women have no rights, they are only there to please the husband and bear children. One hears horror-stories of young brides being burnt alive for not having brought enough dowry.;- of sisters being married to the Koran, for not having to share the land for her dowry;- of couples being locked into a room together, therefore giving an excuse to kill them for immorality, just to get rid of an enemy. Of course Women being killed after being raped, because they have brought shame on the family, while the male gets away scot-free. No need to say that there are laws against all these evils, but what law? In these parts of the country the big landowners make the law, the poor people are uneducated and the police is mostly corrupt, therefore offenders are never found and prosecuted. It will need some time yet to get rid of all these bad practices.

Customs

The birth of a baby is everywhere in the world a big event. In Muslim society a woman is supposed to stay at home for 40 days after delivery. This is of course not adhered to any more. Already most babies of the middle class are born in hospitals, and poor women have to earn their living. If possibly babies are breastfed, and that for as long as 2 years. Unfortunately modern advertising is tempting young mothers who want to be up to date, to feed with the bottle. Some uneducated mothers from the lower class of society also start to bottle-feed, to be able to leave the baby at home, while they are working. But as milk, and especially baby milk is expensive, they keep the half-empty bottle for the next feed. Without refrigerator, and in a hot climate the milk gets spoiled, and sometimes babies even die of the consequences. I remember a court case, which was highly advertised, against Nestlé for advertising their milk as equal to breast milk, therefore misleading some mothers to change from breast feeding.

Children are constantly looked after and carried around. They sleep with the mother for the first years, mostly until the next baby arrives. Solids are started when the child is ready to digest- - a bit of rice, some fruit, and some pounded meat. There are no readymade baby foods available .

The Islamic law is, that for every son, one should distribute the meat of two goats to the poor, for daughters one goat. This has to be done before the age of forty, therefore allowing a respite for poor people. As one third of the meat can be kept, this is usually an occasion for relatives to celebrate.

Marriages are very elaborate. They are also the bane of the society.

One week before the marriage ceremony, the bridegroom's family visits the bride. They bring a shalwar-kamise dress in yellow color and some necklace and bangles made from flowers. After this the young girl is not supposed to leave the house. This also is not followed anymore, more likely the girl has an appointment with the hairdresser or the tailor just before the wedding day. The evening before the wedding is the « Mehndi » celebration. The whole family gets together; the idea is to put Mehndi, which is Henna on the bride's hands and feet. This is done by the female relatives of the bridegroom. In modern houses it is just a kind of pretense. There have to be a certain number of females, maybe 10,I do not remember, who take a little of the paste to stain the bride's hand , but the girl keeps a paper handkerchief in her hand, to avoid staining the palm, which is later adorned by professionals with very beautiful designs. Her hair also has to be oiled, this is also done in a symbolical fashion, by dipping one finger into the oil, and hardly touching the hair of the bride. After this ceremony is completed, the young girls and women sit together on a carpet with the « dolki » (drum). They sing wedding songs. Very often there are competitions between the two parties, bride's vs. bridegroom's. This used to be a women only affair, but these days everybody enjoys. The well-to-do often hire bands to play and sing, and the young people dance. There is of course an elaborate meal for everybody, mostly well over 100 people. This is an occasion which I enjoyed always, the dances, the song competitions, and of course the beautiful dresses and jewelries of the guests; a sparkling affair.

On the actual wedding day the bride is sent to a beautician for her makeup and hairstyling. The « Barat » (the bridegroom with all his followers) arrives in a decorated car, together with his friends and family. Firstly the « Nikkah »(wedding vows) is performed, signatures are exchanged. Then there is the wedding meal: rice, roast chicken, three to four different meat-curries, fruit, and sweet dishes, served with soft drinks for around 200 persons or more.

After the meal the bride is brought in. She is of course dressed in a very beautiful wedding dress, mostly in red, with gold embroidery. Quite often bride and bridegroom used to see each other for the first time, sometimes in a mirror held before them. This is so because the majority of marriages are still arranged. But customs are loosening up, and lots of families allow their daughters to at least meet the chosen young man after the engagement. This type of marriage has as much chance to succeed those love-marriages, because there are not too many expectations, and both parties try to adapt to each other. But mostly it is the girl who has to change her habits, as she enters into the family of her husband.

The car of the newlywed is decorated with flowers. Sometimes it is even a beautiful horse cart to take the bride away. In the villages the bridegroom arrives on a white horse, accompanied by a wedding band, which makes a terrible noise.

The day after the wedding is the « Valima », that is the only ceremony prescribed by Islam, the rest are customs taken over from the Indian Hindus. This is a meal given to all the relatives, to announce the wedding, and therefore the entry of a new woman into the family. Again the sumptuous meal, as very often both families try to outshine each other.

I am of course describing here customs in well to do families. But quite often less rich people, for appearance sake go along with all that. If one considers, that most of the family stays for up to three days ,the young sleeping on mats on the floor, the elders put up with neighbors, or sometimes in hotels, one can well imagine the cost of all this. On top of this comes the dowry. The bride is supposed to receive all the necessary for starting a new household: furniture, crockery, beddings, electric appliances etc. Also expensive dresses, and gold jewelry. Very often the well-to-do give a car, or even a plot or a house. The bridegroom also receives an expensive watch and a few suits of clothes. Even the mother in law and sisters in law expect some small gold trinkets. The mother gets usually bangles.. There are also suit pieces to be given for all the uncles and aunts, brothers, sisters and cousins; usually that amounts to a few dozens of suit-pieces. Of course this depends on your fortune, but what I know, that it is always more than one can actually afford. Quite a lot of families are ruined by the marriage of their daughters. It is however custom to give money as wedding present by the relatives, which helps a bit, a kind of loan to be returned at a future marriage in the family of the donor.

The customs around death also involve the whole family. If someone dies, the family has to be informed immediately, because the burial has to take place within 24 hours. Everyone arrives at the house of the deceased, and prayers are performed. There is usually loud wailing by the closest members of the family. Only the men go to the cemetery. The body is washed and then wrapped in the burial sheets. No casks are used.

In the house where someone has died, custom forbids to light a fire for three days. Therefore the relatives bring the food. Usually big cooking pots of rice are prepared, serving around 60, and some simple meat curry with it. The family of the deceased is accompanied for forty days. Almost every afternoon some female relatives arrive to help out, and once a week there are prayers.

You see, without the family nothing goes in Pakistan.

The Eids

Eid are the Moslem festivals, they could well be compared to Christmas and Easter, as for their importance in the life of the family. The first Eid is called the sweet Eid. It comes after the 30 days of fasting during the Ramadan. As the Muslim months coincide with the moon, everybody goes out of the house on the eve of Eid to see the new moon. For this Eid everybody wears new clothes, especially the children. The night before the festival shops are open almost the whole night. Women go out to buy sweets and glass bangles and the bazaars are lit and decorated.

The morning of the big day everyone gets up early. The men prepare themselves to go to the mosque for the special prayer, while the women start cooking. Women are also allowed to go to the mosque for prayers, contrary to the believe of some, but it is not obligatory, as it is for the men. Some homemade sweet dishes are sent to all the neighbors with wishes for a nice day. Children put on their fineries, ready to see their friends. They are also eager to wish « Eid Mubarik » to parents and grandparents, from whom they can expect some pocket money. This festival lasts two days, and families get together for at least one meal.

The second Eid comes after the completion of Hadj or pilgrimage. Every Muslim, who can afford it, is supposed to sacrifice a goat or sheep and distribute 2/3 of the meat to the poor. This is to commemorate the sacrifice of the Prophet Abraham , who had to scarify a lamb instead of his son. The needy go from house to house where goats have been slaughtered to collect meat, which they cook or dry. Sometimes the Eid days are the only ones during the year, when these people can eat meat. The whole thing is a bloody affair, and really was never to my liking. Here also the family gathers for a feast once in the three holidays. Mostly one day is spent with the family of the husband, the other with that of the wife.

Social System

The social system in Pakistan is actually the family. The Government has once introduced a pension scheme for private business. Government employees were already covered by this. Maybe in big factories it is in place, but I remember, that among the 25 or so employees of my husband, only two wanted to join. The others absolutely refused. Maybe they did not trust the government to pay them later on. Also I remember that one big businessman in Faisalabad built an old age home out of a trust. This was standing empty for some years, until it was turned into a children's hospital, Nobody wanted to send their old parents to such a place.

The family is the big social insurance here. Students live with their parents until they get a job, and mostly until they get married. Joint family system is still very common, where all the married sons get one or two rooms in the same house with the parents. This of course breeds differences, but has its advantages as well. If a woman chooses to work, which is still not common practice, there is always someone to look after the children. The parents also are provided for, once they can no more earn their living.

Parents are responsible for the education of their children. This can be quite a financial load, as private schools and colleges are not cheap. But later the sons look after the financial needs of the parents.

Daughters are given a dowry, which is quite considerable, but on the death of the parents they get only one part of the inheritance, against two for the sons.

Wives inherit 1/8 of the fortune. The rest is divided into one part for each daughter, and two for each son. At the same time it is the sons who are responsible for aging parents. If a male member of the family dies, it is common for the rest of the family to support the widow and children as well as possible. Male members of a family bear quite a lot of responsibility, while the ladies are mostly housewives « only ».

This works quite well, but of course there is a continuous dependence on one's family.

Education

The government program for schooling is five years for primary education, eight for middle standard and ten for Matriculation. Primary is actually obligatory, but for whatever reason this has never been implicated. The literacy-rate in Pakistan is to my knowledge less than 50%. In class six starts English as a second language. Matriculation exams can be passed in Urdu or English standard.

Most of the private schools are English medium schools. They were mainly missionary schools some decades ago, but now there are lots of Elite schools, some even from American or British school systems.

In the villages there are schools without proper buildings. The teacher sits with his pupils under a tree, to avoid the blazing sun. He has to teach all primary classes together. Secondary classes from fifth to eight are in bigger neighboring villages.

Quite a lot of people send their children to « Madrassas », that is Koran-schools, where they learn to read and write and some mathematics, apart from religious studies. Most of these schools are quite moderate, and they fill a vacuum for poor people, therefore allowing children to get some basic education, who otherwise would not have the opportunity. Some of these Madrassas, unfortunately, misuse their power to breed fanatics, but they are really in a minority. This has to be said once, as here in the West people believe, that all Koran schools breed terrorism.

In the English Medium schools kids learn Urdu and English at the same time. That is not at all easy, as Urdu is written in the Arabic script. Therefore the little scholars have to learn two alphabets at the same time. The advantage is, that by the time they absolve their Matriculation, they speak English fluently. This is a big plus, as all further education in Colleges and Universities is in English. But Urdu schools also bring forth excellent pupils. My four son-in-laws were students of Urdu Medium, and they are all in leading positions now.

More and more students nowadays opt for O-Levels instead of Matriculation, and A-Levels instead of BA or BSC. (Batchelor of Arts or Science) So they have an internationally acknowledged degree, and it is also easier to get admission into the Universities. There are now American and British Universities in Pakistan, but not many people can afford those, the fees are adapted to standards in their own countries, i.e. 60 Rs for a Dollar. The only advantage lies in young people not to have to go abroad for further studies.

Health system

In Pakistan there is no proper health system as such. There are hospitals for the poor, where for a few pence they can get a consultation, and supposedly free medication. But the expensive medicines are usually not available, because very often, they have been sold by the staff to the drugstores.

Government officials and army personnel have right to free medical care.

But there are lots of doctors who have opened their small clinics in the streets and bazaars of the towns. They are the general practitioners who serve the majority of the population. Usually there is a small waiting room, often divided by a curtain for women and men, a small examination room with a table, a few chairs and an examination table. Here the doctors have to see a few dozen of patients every evening, with hardly any modern equipment. For x-rays or blood examinations the patients are sent to laboratories, which are usually in the vicinity. There are

Assistants, called compounders, who prepare simple medicines, pounding and mixing tablets into powder; they also give injections. The more elaborate medicines have to be bought in the drugstores, and are very expensive, like everywhere in the world. Therefore these doctors have to make do with very basic drugs, and very often antibiotics are used. As the majority of people are barely educated, I believe these doctors prefer to prescribe injections, maybe to avoid wrong dosages? These simple medical men are the backbone of the Pakistani health system, and they are doing a wonderful job. Hampered by lack of time (not more than 5 minutes per patient) and lack of modern equipment, they take care, for little money, of all the poor and quite a lot of the middle class. These are the doctors who treated me and my children, and I believe I never had any bad experience.

There is of course the problem of the injections:

Before the disposable syringes were available, the assistant had to inject an average of 10 people per hour. The needles used to be in continuously boiling water, which was not enough to sterilize them. Therefore illnesses like hepatitis were spread just by these clinics. Also, due to the shyness of some female patients, who did not want to bare their buttocks, injections were applied through the cloth of their shalwars!

Another problem is the unqualified « doctors ». They are tolerated, because of the lack of properly qualified men. They manage quite nicely for common fevers and colds, and can so take the load off the general practitioners, but as they are not formed for proper examinations, they often give the wrong drugs. Some are clever enough to send such sick people to proper doctors, but unfortunately not all.

Of course there are all the specialists. They sit in more elaborate and modern clinics. Often a few get together to open private hospitals, which are gold-mines. Most of them work in the government hospitals as well for a few hours per week.

In the hospitals there is always a lack of nurses. Every patient has to have an attendant from his family for small cares. Also no food is served, therefore a sick person requests quite a lot of coming and going to and from the hospital, food has to be brought, medicines have to be bought and attendants change shifts.

Pakistani doctors are well qualified, and lots of them work in UK and USA, but most of the modern apparatus available in the West is lacking. Unfortunately, no sickness insurance being available, the poor have not much access to the specialists.

Politics

I must firstly say that I understand nothing about politics, and am, frankly told not very interested. Also I am aware, that I must be a bit brain-washed, having been exposed to Pakistani newspaper reports and Television. But I also know, that the West has an entirely wrong view of politics in Eastern countries. Democracy, as we luckily know it in Europe can not really succeed in underdeveloped countries. The public is mostly totally unaware what politic is concerned. They will vote for their landlords, because they have to, if they do not want to lose their livelihood. And then these very landlords, who are not at all qualified to rule a country, do nothing but enrich themselves, caring not a hoot for Pakistan and its people. I have lived through so many different elected governments and quite a few Marshall Laws as well. I sincerely feel that the periods under the army were the more progressive ones. This is so, because even democratically elected Presidents tend to become dictators. Like the saying:
» Power corrupts, and absolute power corrupts absolutely. »

In general the people are happy if they are allowed to earn a decent living, and they do not really care who is at the helm.

But of course every few years the opposition is stirring up trouble to get a chance to lead.

Mr.Bhutto was the first really democratic elected leader. He promised the workers « roti, kapra or makan » what means bread, clothes and a house. He also promised to distribute the land of the rich to the poor. When he came to power he did distributed lots of land to the poor, but only the land of his opponents. He was one of the biggest landowners of Sindh, but I never heard of him giving anything away. His rule was also one of the worst, he installed most modern torture-chambers under the old fort in Lahore, where anyone daring to oppose him could be tortured. So much for democracy!

I personally only hope, that the Islamists will not succeed in ruling Pakistan, as then I would be really worried about my children and grandchildren, but I do not believe that the people will let that happen. Pakistan is really a moderate Muslim state.

As I say, this is Pakistan as I see it, after nearly 40 years of living in a Middle class family. I might be wrong, and other people might have a different opinion, but this is my and my family's Pakistan.